A Bear in the Kitchen

New and Collected Poems

By Michael Salinger

red giant
books

Copyright © 2013 Michael Salinger

A Bear in the Kitchen
New and Collected Poems

Cover design by Zachary Skalko

Author photo by Rai Collins

Author website: www.michaelsalinger.com

Red Giant Books
ISBN: 978-0-9883430-3-0

10 9 8 7 6 5 4 3 2 1

Printed in the United States of America.

www.redgiantbooks.com

Table of Contents

Table of Contents (con't)

A Borrowed Cabin

You don't want a bear in the kitchen
they make a terrible mess
so said the neighbor on the phone
a tiny electronic voice of caution
whose ring we almost didn't answer
because we were so sure it couldn't be for us
this not being our home
> *it's not their fault, you see*
> *they are so hungry*
> *this time of year*
> *having drowsed through most of the winter and all*
> *and this one's pretty aggressive*
> *busted right into the house*
> *across the creek from you*
> *be careful*

What does one do?
when ones place in the food chain
has been threatened
by 328 pounds of groggy
louse infested Ursus Americanus
claws capable of raking through
a refrigerator's skin
as easily as if it were the cake's frosting
the beast smells hidden behind
magnetic weather-stripped doors
canines the size of a human forefinger
implanted in jaws endowed
with twelve hundred pound per square inch
bite force
tiny squares of glistening safety glass
from an exploded patio door
diamond dusted into matted fur
sparkling like snowflakes

in the silent moonlight
do you go onto the deck?
beat pans and pots together
turn off the lights
hide in the closet amongst the snowshoes
do you pray?
and to whom
what does one do?
when reason
and logic
and your master's degree
in 16th century literature
are rendered useless
by a confused and frightened carnivore
scratching at
the kitchen door?

Wading

The ducks are laughing at us
quacking green headed maniacs
we in our rubber waders
thigh-deep in gin clear river flow
vacuum compressed
shrink wrapped cool against legs

leafs balance on surface tensed finger tips
afraid to get their bellies wet
conveyor belt riding the stream
while auburn autumn sun glows lukewarm at treetop
and these Manistee strain steelheads
couldn't be less impressed with our spinners
egg sacks, jigs and maggots
or anything else we decide to throw

and a river is nothing but a waterfall
laying on its back
current passing by
steady and slow pooling in the flats
swirling into eddies
behind fallen tree trunks and rocks
tumbling through riffles and rapids
pouring past my son and me
350 cubic feet per second
never to return to this spot again

walking against the current
is every bit as hard as they say
and silt will swallow a leg
like wet cement
green Ohio slate is slippery
and the water is invariably deeper than it looks
and sometimes you have to carry
a boy across a river

when his boots aren't tall enough
and both are for left feet
'cause his mom got them on sale
and this young man will
cling to you like a laboratory monkey
wriggle
spook and jerk
knocking you off balance
while you wade across
and you'll nearly fall
more times than the boy will ever know
or you will ever care to tell him

'cause the day will come
when you'll let him lead
search out his own path across
not worried anymore that he'll drown
so that
when he slips and falls
you'll know to go around
thinking to yourself
better him than me

Frankie's Poem

Storm clouds of baitfish
dart in Jungian schools
scales sparking silver
like lightning flashes
slipping en masse
through river smoothed rocks
The herons are acting crazy today
you said
and you were right
squawking over fishing spots
with less composure than a crow
dog fighting
through the tops of bank rooted willows
with the grace
of a catapulted
55 gallon drum
branches and leaves splashing
below
the victor returns
staring with pickax determination
into the water flowing past
its stilted legs
as still as the stuffed specimen
you saw on fifth grade field trip
to natural history museum
till it jabs its needle bill
into the current
with the speed of a sewing machine
coming up

       empty

and we laugh
you in red day camp shirt

summer buzz cut
and glasses repaired on the ride out
you say that I ought to write a poem
about herons not catching fish
with every try
trying to distract me
while I untangle the explosion
of braided nylon bird nested around your reel
I retie a swivel and spinner
to your line
you cast upstream
this day holding all the promise
of a brand new lure.

Belay Off

Belay off
They tell you to never look down
The average climbing rope is 50 meters long
and rated by the number of falls
it can withstand
because
it is expected that you are going to lose your grip
And these ropes are designed to stretch
up to 6.5% of their length
thus
absorbing your body's weight
as it accelerates
thirty two point one eight feet
per second per second
spring-backing you to a stop
rather than snapping you in half

But with a carabineer click
you've unhooked yourself
Belay off
And up you scale
chalk absorbs hand sweat
but not your fingertip pain
Trigger loaded cams
sway at your waist
like a cluster of colored pendulums
picked one by one
inserted into fissures and cracks
then left behind
as if they were antique keys
poking from an attic's trunk
And you look up
because you've been warned to never look down
feeling for imperfections in the rock

facilitating enough friction
that you may cling to its face
as you surmount this obstacle
One hand
      One foot
            At a time
Simply
      Because
            It is there
And once you've reached the summit
before you spy your next climb
go ahead
look down
See how far you've come

Belay off

For Emily

A wild bird in the house portends bad luck
even death
So said my grandmother
she of Slovenian descent
This superstition though, transcends nationality
migrating across imaginary boundaries demarcating countries
Italians, Greek, Scandinavian, Irish, Chinese
all warn against harboring
undomesticated things with feathers

The cats wake us at sunrise
howling and chasing through the front of the house
and I assume they are fighting
over another imaginary feline slight
Then I recognize
the flutter of wings in distress
so I put on my slippers

The mourning dove shivers
wedged behind the grandfather clock
cat tails twitching with pendulum precision
Feathers littering the room
betray the mayhem that had only just subsided

I eye the bird's beak
thin, pointed, needlelike
weigh the chances of disease
I cup its warm, weightless and hollow boned body
in my hands
pinning its wings with my palms to its side
I open the door with my elbow

I toss the bird into the air

Two Men in a Coffee Shop

God drives a Subaru station wagon
putting on her make-up
reflected in sun visor vanity mirror
three kids in the back seat
and she's going to pull this damn car over
if they don't stop that fighting

The automobile passes a suburban coffee shop
two men inside
smoke cigarettes
laugh too loud
mangle middle aged jokes about golf
they pontificate on sump pumps and tile grout
weather and automobile financing
as if impervious to mortality
Mr. Plumber leaves to cook
breakfast for an aging father
the other
competes with coughin' cappuccino device
cell phoning home to remind flannel pajama 'ed wife
of daughter's soccer practice

I marvel at their heroism
as I am astonished by the infinity
of the ocean of nameless faces
I encounter for the one time in my life
every single day
their ability to remain upright
while wading the current
of daily existence
fully dressed
in invisible clothes
interwoven threads
saturated with the amortized accumulation
of experience

How much easier it would be
to back float
then simply slowly sink
beneath the stream
knees to chest in fetal submission
layered blankets of silt
compressing life's echo into
two dimensional fossil
while overhead
the rest of the world
tow the anchors of
 if only…

How much easier it would be
to stare into the abyss
eyes already shut in preparation
and just wait for the show to end
killing time

But god makes a right on red
and turns into the donut shop
the kids quiet down
in anticipation

Redtail

2900 pounds
of
steel, rubber, fabric
and glass pointed west
driving from cleveland to chicago
a nuclear physicist riding shotgun
Just
In
Case.
Rather than atoms
we split hairs
plucked from the heads
of men half our age.
Philosophizing like students
as we enter the existential state
that is
Indiana.
Not Texas flat
but flat enough
to cause one's eyes to glaze
143 miles of
furrowed brown soil
waiting for this season's seed
Fall by
like primordial spring dominos.
Flat enough
to see thunderheads
stationed
a half hour in the future.
Suspended in the sky
mammoth gray jellyfish
electro static charges bolting
through rain tendrils.
Yet,
we remain dry.

Rolling by
metronome telephone poles,
the horizon
as linear and truth laden as time -
spiked by
silos, barns, farmhouses
and juvenile red-tailed hawks
training to hunt
by hopping
from bark covered fencepost.

Occasionally we see
a tree -
trunk spared from saw
stump from TNT
standing solo sentry
in freshly tilled
soy bean field
cultivated earth flowing
over and past
buried roots
   Imagine
   a photograph of river water
   flowing around boulder
left to the
bonsai twisting whim
of weather.
While seasons pass
like passengers in chartered bus
headed to Indian casino.

These trees
owing existence
to lack of utility.
Too quick burning for fuel
soft for table or chair
crooked for beam or floorboard

just as easy to plow around
not worth removal's effort.
Thus
cambium rings
a silent repository of history.

The car's front end
sword swallows the road before us.
Nothin' but gray skies,
black asphalt highway sensation
plunger in trombone bell
muted
by tire, shocks and struts.
Stan Getz's ghost blowing
through radio's speaker
precipitating notes in between

Tall and Tan and Young and Lovely

The physicist tells me of his visit
to Ipanema
where the words for bikini
and dental floss are synonymous.
And I imagine half naked
hygienist instructing me to spit, please.
In the left corner of the sky
a hawk's square winged
silhouette draws searchlight circles
atop an updraft
at 33-1/3 revolutions
per minute.
Effortless,
defying the gravity
that keeps turnpike traffic
Earth bound
and men's souls
rooted in the ground.

Neon

A poem is a 1957 Greyhound bus
front tires balloon push wedged up against the curb
diesel engine idle vibrating the rear view mirrors
so that the images within them blur
pneumatically, mnemonically opening the door to individual
interpretation
A poem can be a pair of wingtips
exhausted leather shoes,
or an angel's feathers
either image will do (it's just a transit token coin flip)
But, take these wingtips
and like a sacrificial pawn
center them on a square of scuffed linoleum tile
part of a pattern chess boarding across the floor
of some Podunk town's art deco bus terminal
cruciform-cracked plaster arching overhead
the whole effigy
bustin' up the sunsank horizon of your experiences
with the blue
transformational hum of phosphorescent neon

A poem can be the outdated pack of Twizzlers
in the silver pull knobbed candy machine
that you contemplate trading your last two quarters for
when you are starving to death
Or a poem can be that stale cup of coffee
on Formica counter at 3am
in front of the only occupied stool
at the end of a chrome and red vinyl mushroom line
when your dreams make you afraid
to close your eyes and go to sleep

A poem could be warp and woof weaved
inside the gray cotton ball puffs

exhaling from a black tail pipe into subzero air
as internal combustion revs in response
to the depression of an accelerator
lurching away from a Plexiglas shelter
accordion doors playing a traveling tune
as they fold closed

Or
a poem can smell
like burning rubber
When the accumulated slush
that has built up within the wheel well of your mind
has solidified into ice
grasping your spinning tires
in expanding frigid vice
'til you can't go any further

You just can't go any further
'til you risk your life
pulling off to the side of the road
kicking the obstruction to the median
the rest of the world becoming the breeze of
semi-trucks roaring by
then you pull away
dissolving into the arterial rush of traffic
leaving the clump behind
to become a reflection that is closer than it appears
which will melt with the next thaw
depositing salt bleached bits of gravel
in an indecipherable
I Ching formation
That nonetheless confirms
you were there

A poem can just as easily
take you
to
or away
from home

Even Though the Bus is Late

It's time
I have been away so long
and now I am coming home
to you
more migration's completion than journey's end
inevitable as high tide covering water's mark on pier and rock
impelled by a gravity distant, constant as the moon
an orbit closing
full circle
I am coming home
having been away for so long
from you
I have less choice
than the gravid fish impelled by natal river scent
thunder's pursuing clap
or the cicada clawing from the soil after seventeen years
to split its translucent amber shell before setting wings to air
I am coming home
with so much to share
with you
and
nothing will stop me.

"German nursing homes started a trend that has taken hold of European nursing homes throughout the country: fake bus stops for Alzheimer's patients

How the system works is that the bus stop diffuses the sense of panic. For instance, if a delusional patient decided that she needed to go home immediately because her children were all alone and waiting for her, the attendant didn't need to restrain her or talk her out of it, she simply said, "Oh, well, there's the bus stop." Thus, the patient would go sit and wait. Knowing that she was on her way home, she would relax and, given her diminished cognition, she would eventually forget why she was there. Staff can then approach the patients and tell them that the bus is delayed and invite them in for refreshments while they wait. Five minutes later they have completely forgotten they wanted to leave."

"Fake Bus Stops For Alzheimer's patients in Germany" International Association of Chiefs of Police. 2011. http://www.theiacp.org/About/Governance/Divisions/StateAssociationsofChiefsofPoliceSACOP/CurrentSACOPProjects/MissingAlzheimersDiseasePatientInitiative/AlzheimersSuccessStory/tabid/1007/Default.aspx?id=1665

Chicago

A couple coins
next to a cherry scented Para dichlorobenzene
disinfectant block atop a plastic screen
in an O'Hare airport urinal
does not a wishing well make.

Luck and betrayal are cousins
mercifully
eventually
doses of either
run out.

Esprit D'Escalier

one begins wearing a watch
becomes serious
as gradually
as one realizes
the gravity of time.
one cannot hold one's breath
'til death by suffocation
without the employment
of some outside mechanism.

Capitulation

My cats hate me
and I truly believe
they actively plot
against me

Nowadays,
going underground
is leaving my cell phone home
I've been known to drink coffee
too late at night
in spite of myself

Sometimes life is like
walking into a fire hose
full blast
other times
                                    it's not

Plecostomus

A Pleco
is a good fish to have
in an aquarium
they work the night shift
in the dark
cleaning up messes

One night
I flickered on the fluorescent light
it flashed
like far away lightning
and I caught him
his suction cup mouth
attached to the waterlogged carcass
of a recently deceased
tiger barb
like shredded cotton wadding
the pleco slowly
inhaling the entire mass
just on the edge of perception

It was like
accidently interrupting your mother
while she chowed down on a human forearm
illuminated by 3am refrigerator light

You never talk about it
your eyes meet
and something passes
a silent conversation transmits
via mutually embarrassed glances
    an understanding
        that some things
            just take too long to explain

Stingray

The young man believed
he had hooked an angel
shark
line ripping from his bait casting reel
drag click whizzing away like
a New Year's Eve noisemaker
attached to an electric drill
the rest of the anglers
at his end of the pier
grabbing their gear
clearing way
to watch this fight
big fish
big fish

big fish on
passes
      tide steady
down 600 foot fishing pier
as tackle lay abandoned
on weather cured planks
so that the owners
could catch this show

50 pound test line
stretching tight
guttural cat howling
like an out of tune violin
while the young man
repels down a mountainside
back leaning with all his weight
gaining three feet
giving up
two

towed from one roughhewn railing
to the other
for three tortuous quarters of an hour
before we even see
the fish

rolling near the surface
like a king sized sheet
flashing by
in a washing machine
filled with dark green ink
the white underside
of a 150 lb. sting ray
slicing by for a fraction of eternity
then diving as if sucked down a drain
fiberglass composite rod
broomstick thick
arches downward
toward the moon's reflected
static scribbled across the waves
twenty feet below the pier
a catapult
the instant before sword
slices rope
and our guy is hanging tight
and time stops
        and solidifies
like the briny residue of sea spray
crystallizing in the corner of one's mouth
while we wait
seconds tick tick ticking away
each of us expecting
the line to snap

but he's hanging tight
when most would have cut it loose by now
a sting ray is a garbage fish after all
not fit for food

too expensive for taxidermist's bench
but it's become a matter of principle
to the kid
and finally
the rod slowly unbends
like an arching dinosaur's neck
the fish breaks the surface
and surrenders

a giant three pronged gaffing hook
attached to tire swing thick rope
pulls the fish up
dripping
like a Volkswagen being lifted
from a farm pond by crane
three men haul it over the railing
drop it on the deck
slick white belly up
blood spatter illuminated by mercury vapor
softball size mouth full of pointed teeth
gasping in the terrible air

and

the first baby was a surprise
like a black dinner plate
gliding out from under a rug
but four more followed
each
mindful of the stinger
gingerly
tossed back into the sea
by astonished fishermen
then the mother is heaved over
smacking the water spread eagle flat
with the sound of
tree split by lightening cracking
predator attracting blood

billowing wake trailing her escape
her offspring
fish born out of water
fly in formation
oblivious to the sacrifice

Heron

The Great Blue Heron does not flock
its caste is that of a loner
shadowing the river's edge
long neck hunched into shoulders
caught in a snapshot
of a whip
on the back swing
Undertaker solemn demeanor
reed thin limbs wade through the shallow
with calculated giant steps
webbed toes incising the water's surface
with the choreographed precision
of slow motion pistons
Translucence lapping into invisibility
dissolving into the landscape
and passing by
immutable as the second hand on a clock

The younger boy quit baiting his hook a half hour ago
casting the red and white bobber upstream into the current
trailing crescent of line
refracting sunrise through prisms
of water droplets
clinging to the braided nylon
Then Frankie watches the hollow globe of plastic drift by
empty hook beneath
his eyes fixed
repressing a smile during this serious business
'til the stream stretches it taught
and he cranks on the reel
tick tick ticking to start over again
And I encourage this behavior
in seven year old boys
with summertime Curious George haircuts

while I coach his older brother's use
of my spinning rod
and in the intricacies of top water
smallmouth bass fishing

And the moment of a memory is that Great Blue Heron
camouflaged to float into the everyday
like the metallic murmur of cicadas
only made apparent by absence
so that staring into the bird's eyes
we still just see
        a corrugated drain pipe
                cattails and clamshells
                        a carp skeleton
                                picked clean

And I tell the boys
that their great grandfather used to say
"They call it fishing not catching"
Dropping the allure of the day
where experience tells me a fish could be
hoping to stamp this instant in their minds
manufacture a memory
But still the most sublime cast is rarely
met with success
even at six thirty
in the morning
before the sun's heat
evaporates
dew drops and good intention

And I wonder if the image of fishing
will take within Frankie
all elbows and knees, ball cap and tank top
or will he recollect me
wrenching him off the power line's shadow tightrope
that he followed absentmindedly
from the parking lot of the drugstore

into the street
The yellow imprint of my right hand
sinks into the skin of his warm summer arm
engulfed by the wake
of blood return
plotting the blueprint
of a bruise that may
or may not fade
away.

Glasses

At least I had enough sense
to lock my floating Flambeau ™ tackle box
while I wishbone straddle balanced on the edges of my canoe
Jack Nicholson ax swinging an oar above my head
in a futile attempt to dislodge
the $3.85 Jitterbug lure that my cretinous brother in law
had managed to feed the catalpa tree
Leafs and twigs rain down onto the water's surface
concentric circles outlining their landings
swelling and enveloping each other
in desktop feng shui rake patterns
An animated Tibetan meditation icon
an aquatic mandala – if you will
whose hypnotic grasp is only broken
by the splash
of a 6'1", 200lb. male that just happened to be me

The evening sky rolled by in a hard banking turn'
as the boat obeyed the laws Newton
back slamming beneath the surface of the water
wherein I discovered the true absorbency of my flannel shirt
and the exact depth of the silt on the pond's bottom
The electric thrill of oxygen deprivation
races the water that is filling my ears, eyes and throat
and I am six years old
and I'm in my back yard
and my old man
he's holding me under the water
He thinks it's a joke
but it's not funny anymore
I can't breath
it's just not funny anymore
Until finally my murky shadow burst from the water
and like a sea lion coughing of the coast of Alcatraz

I wade to the shore and I discover
I don't have my glasses anymore.

Everything is fuzzy
all the sharp edges
the coloring book outlines
they've slipped away
like the scales from Saul turned Paul's eyes
I've crawled from this primordial soup into
a brand new impressionistic world
While a large mouthed bass
he's starting his life anew
wearing my glasses
a fresh water version of the Amazing Mr. Limpit
warning his cohorts that,
"Hey Hey Hey Buddy – get away from there – that's just a lure!"
But I don't know the difference anymore
'cause everything is soft – everything is safe
I'm living in a foam rubber landscape
Oncoming semi-truck headlights
those are just big happy fireflies
and the bathroom tiles seem to be cruising around the room
In fact 99.9 percent of all inanimate objects are really alive
And I realize
with my real eyes
Salvador Dali – he was a photographer
At least I had enough sense to lock my tackle box
and nowadays
if you got the scoots
you can get new glasses in an hour.

Flotsam

My thoughts are not so deep
anymore
like a tide ebbing
their surfaces steadily receding
drawn away from shore
by the constituents of my life
my son at university
his excogitations swim
Kierkegaardian shark circles
dorsal fins slicing the surf
snapping the backs of schooling ideas
with a confident head shake
swallowed in chunks
by rows of replenishable teeth
shards of flesh and scale
left in his wake
while
my boats lay listing in mud
moored to piers casting shadows across their decks
an insurance bill flops about exposed rocks
gills breathing in the terrible oxygen
oystercatchers loud and obvious
stab thick orange beaks at aspirations
hunkered in their shells
gelatinous globs of amorphous phylum
slowly dehydrate in the evening sun
further down the beach
washed up
carried by current from depths that never knew light
a giant squid
milky eye the size of a full moon on the horizon
will be collected by Japanese scientist
studied and dissected
wherein they will find
the half-digested body
of a great white

Vespula Vulgaris

The boy paid no particular attention
to the pear tree that he hid behind
sprawling branches
twisted above his head
or the legion of
yellow jacket wasps
buzzing in drunken circles
around fallen
fermenting summertime fruit
turning brown on the ground
nor did he bother to contemplate
the rough reptilian bark slipping beneath
tufts of grass becoming root
nerve tendril clutching the earth like
wooden shocks of lightening
frozen in time
the fact that he had
his father's chin, his grandfather's wit
his mother's almond eyes
his brother's Swiss army knife
illicitly in his pocket
and the family posture
shoulders sloped as if by weight
never crossed his mind
the boy did not notice the curl of dust
kicked from behind automobile
headed to horizon
the driver in yellow sundress
determined to escape
and never come back this time
or the whistle of the gopher
startled by the car's passing
a full moon
cut from translucent tissue

still visible in the daytime sky
went equally ignored
the flash of slick tanned skin
of black haired
neighbor girl
skinny-dipping
had become the entire universe
to him

Time is a great teacher, but unfortunately it kills all its pupils.
Hector Louis Berlioz

Nietzsche's Horse

At thirteen
my son,
his body a coat hanger
jutting from a tank top
and baggy shorts,
wants to comprehend
only one thing -
that being,
everything

His mother speaks of gardening
and seeds
because that is what she knows

I lecture on trajectory
the speed of sound sluicing through liquid
baseball analogies
economics
Newton's third law of physics
and plumbing fixtures
because I know nothing
all the time swearing
that what I know
is best

He sits
back against checkered tile wall,
in an armless wooden kitchen chair
part of the set
that his mother and I bought
before we split
I think it is made from maple,

waiting for the answers
to the questions
that keep me awake

I do not say
that truth comes as a dream
details fading with sunrise
or that the miracle of life
is the tribulation that we survive
Rather, I assure him
that in time he will understand
hoping
that'll hold him
for a while.

Parochial Education

When I was in first grade
clip on tied and cowlicked
front teeth seemingly the size of slide projector screens
going to Catholic school
we were given these insurance sheets
opportunities for our parents to benefit financially
from our unexpected death or dismemberment
Sister Mary Imelda would pass out these fliers
pewter crucifix pendulum swaying around her neck
"oldest and only please"
and we were supposed to take these brochures home
in a yellow bus riding bundle
along with our H.R. Pufnstuf tin lunchboxes
and gym clothes that needed washing
some church affiliated agency
the Cleveland diocese had a newspaper too
the Universe Bulletin
they sent us door to door
hawking subscriptions to the Universe Bulletin
as if anyone really wanted to subscribe
an early lesson in humility
and failure
I always did much better
with the Christmas cards, holiday candles and chocolate bars
anyway
on these glossy insurance sheets were listed cash rewards
for the loss of various body parts
like one of those charts you see
at the butcher shop
dotted lines demarcating a flank steak
or rump roast
we could see what we were worth
the list of payouts scheduled ala Carte
loss of index finger or thumb $2,500.00

any of the other fingers $1,600.00
eyesight in one eye $5,200.00
the accidental chopping off of a hand $5,000.00
one leg $5,500.00
two legs $10,000.00
all the bits and pieces assigned their numeric value
culminating with loss of life
a cool fifty grand
now I don't recall if I wondered
why my parents had sent me to such a dangerous place
whether I became a little more careful
when closing my desktop
or what my 7-year-old brain (no value attached to it)
shopped for as I perused the list
a mini bike for a ring finger on my left hand perhaps?
I've only just rediscovered this scene
right now
four decades later
but I'm sure
subconsciously
it's had some sort of lasting effect

Cicadas

So thick
they were snow shoveled
from the sidewalks on Public Square
my grandfather called them Canadian soldiers
but the thumb sized black and green bugs
hadn't flown across lake Erie
they clawed up from the soil
after a seventeen year sleep
claim staking the world
for ten summer days
filling the stagnate air with static

then they died

leaving
empty shells
translucent chrysalis
split along the back
clinging to the trees
and brick wall
their bodies crunching underfoot
and bus tire
downtown in front of Higbee's Department Store
a doorman in a red coat
yellow trim at the cuffs
polished shoes
clears the entry
scrape of steel on concrete
white swath cutting through
buzz clicking mass
as if shaving a living beard
years ago
back when
playing with mercury

on the black and white checkered
asbestos tiled kitchen floor
was not yet
dangerous.

Chevy Van

It's a nineteen hundred and eighty Chevy van
brown and white and yellow and tan
since me and the old man
decided to Frankenstein it back on the road
You see it died
with me at the wheel
an internal shotgun blast exploding in the oil pan
somewhere near East 55th
my ear cowl pressed abstract noise checking
during a 65 mile per hour rod shearing cartwheel
into truck heaven

And so it was towed
back to Dad's
and there it sat
for a year-and-a-half
with a spare
'79 straight six on shopping cart wheels
waiting
for an old man
and a younger man
to find time

Now I don't know a lot about putting motors together
but I'm not afraid of grease
and I'll take anything apart
so I ripped off the grill
threw the radiator on the ground
and the old man looked pleased
We backyard scaffold yanked
the deceased engine
scavenged what we could
setting the lifeless block aside to rest in pieces

Now this is taking weeks

We slide the new motor
me nylon strap staining on the back end into place
him underneath
lining up slots and linkage and gear teeth
and pretty soon we turn the key
and the son of a bitch starts
Maybe a minute or two of smooth idle
pistons valves plugs homemade hung power steering box
tapped re-tapped and tapped again brake calipers
and an automatic transmission with a secret handle
working in unison
an internal combustion with purpose and reason
for a minute or two
then we shut it off
'Cause we don't want to push our luck

Next we attack the van's cancerous skin with sand
special sand
not kiddy sand
that's too smooth
we use special sharp-edged sand
high pressure goggle and glove blowing it through hoses
the old man fiberglass fills these holes and dents
and I sand it away
and he fills
and I sand
and he fills
and I sand
and he fills
and I sand
'Cause you can never sand enough
The gloss of the new paint magnifies the imperfections
but it looks a hell of a lot better than it did

And now it gets me back and forth from the shop
'course the heater don't work
but it ain't winter yet.

Runaway Van

Apparently this vehicle never has rear brakes
a fact
denied
masked
an autocidal tendency repressed
by two discs and four opposed shoes
up front
working overtime
A little pressure maybe some pumping and we
would glide
to a controlled stop
safely
nothing risked
dependable transportation

On the surface she seemed a safe ride
and I was comfortable with this arrangement
four thousand pounds of glass and steel reinforced
complacency
I trusted her with my life

A little extra pressure rumba seat goosing fluid
from the master cylinder
snaking through copper tubes
spider twisted beneath undercarriage
each thrust a bit of slipping juice
through brake line crack
with this bit of pressure the gap grows
unperceived
every time

15 degree isosceles grade
gentle depressions receive no response
multiple foot stomps receive no response

desperate grab for the emergency brain receives
no response
Three foot ditch leap
bi-tired Spanky Spangler Evel Knievel and Super
Dave Osborne
roll caged into one maneuver

AIR BORN
AIR BORN
Look Ma I'm flying
I'm flying

White knuckle navigating
road map veins bursting upon over inflated fore arms
in steering wheel do or die
death grip

LOOK MA I'M FLYING

Wheat field racing through maple saplings
through points of strobe light
flashes
a thousand points of reference
but still
I find the time to count the leaves on the trees
ten thousand thoughts ricochet off the guardrails of my skull
'til finally we stop

Heart yellow moth light bulb bouncing
inside chest
and I've yet to decide
whether this ride
will be worth the mess.

Under Cover

I have forgotten all of my best ideas
this I know for certain
I've watched them escape
expire into the distance
dressed in a radiant splendor
the color of ignorance burning
never turning back to wave goodbye
nor acknowledge that I
had any part in their origin
the instant before I fall asleep
I promise myself not to forget
yet away my bright ideas glide
silent, scentless, utterly unnoticed
by the excitable black and white dog
beatifically snoring at my side
down the hall my notion tiptoes
hanging a right past the kitchen
lacing on a pair of my running shoes
tying a double knot that will require a fork to undo
gently turning the knob of my front door
with the care of a safecracker
escaping into the incessant night
like an embarrassed lover
all because I would rather remain
undercover
than leave the comfort of my bed to take a note

Insomnia

Generally you'll sleep through it
but on occasions of anticipation, heartache
or too much caffeine
you may find yourself lying awake
at 3:25 am and the world is silent
perfectly still longing for sleep
you may hear your heart beat
like the pendulum of a grandfather clock
in the next room
ear pressed against pillow
turned back in
listening
to your own blood flow
its echo the sound of the ocean
in a seashell
then in the distance
timpani drums, hundreds of them
muffled mallets bouncing off skins
like a heavy rain on canvas
marching closer and closer
their rhythms resonating in the pit of your stomach
giving way to the metallic clack and clatter
of steel wheel on rail
and then for an instant
the sky is full of train sound
and you're awake
on this occasion of anticipation, heartache
or too much caffeine
then the wheels surrender
to the rain
and the rain bows to the tympani
And the tympani march away
leaving you with the sound
of the ocean in a seashell
but generally
you'll sleep through it.

Daniel Said

for Daniel Thompson – street poet of Cleveland Ohio

daniel said
a poet dies
every two years in cleveland
ohio
whether they need to or not
some are
double wicked candles
flames meeting in center
coalescing into the blinding glint
of hypodermic needle
to be extinguished and buried on hill
overlooking
bankrupt steel mill
some manufacture
22 caliber chakra escape hatches
blown open for cosmic
ejection seats arcing
over the Detroit Superior Bridge
others merely appear deceased
eyes shut behind horn rims
straitjacketed in academic tweed
riding red radio flyer wagon
rubber removed from tires
so rims sync unerringly
with tenure track
the younger become fodder
shot in the back
by canons
before they learn to run
others succumb to crustaceous parasites
side winding in bloodstream
claws snip ticking at time
as if it were decaying chicken
on fishing line

and right now
somewhere at this very instant
a soul with empty stomach
curls fetal in recessed loading dock
face to wall back
to passersby's in silent apology
While inside
soft shell crab appetizer is served
on cobalt blue triangle china
to corporate suit and trophy wife
while another poet dies
right now somewhere
a man with the mental capacity
of a six year old
hums to himself
on rough wool blanketed cot
Nietzsche staring
at whitewashed cinder blockhouse wall
of another death row
at the exact same second
a wing tipped Brooks Brother's button down
auto executive
crunches numbers trying to decide
whether recall would be more expensive
than surviving families' lawsuit
and another poet dies
right now at this very instant
somewhere a child is being beaten
with an orange extension cord
by a parent that doesn't know
any better
right now
someone is giving up hope
someone does not turn the other cheek
someone doesn't consider
the least of his brothers
someone loses the ability
to believe in anything

and another poet dies
right now somewhere
someone fills grocery bag
with day old donuts
to feed the homeless
passes angelic
through the junkyard debris
ranting elegies to compassion
pisses on the bronze castings
of capitalists that cast away
all humanity's good for nothing

right now
a poet
still famous in the neighborhood
still dear to our hearts
shines his shoes
and prepares to walk
across the sky

Fidel Castro at Birdland

Fidel Castro
playing jazz guitar at Birdland
in New York City
on April 26, 2006
his acoustic guitar made by a Japanese man
living in Brazil
where the mahogany for the neck
of the instrument grew
fingerboard crafted from
imported Indian ebony
the front
Oregon cedar
back and sides
the wood of
trumpet shaped blue flowered
jacaranda tree
the machine head
ivory tipped peg and gear assembly
holding eight strings
in tune
precision fabricated in Japan
by computer numerical controlled lathe
and Fidel Castro is singing in Portuguese
laughing at his own lyrics
his left hand crab crawling
up and down the frets
his right bouncing about the strings
as if he were counting the notes
on an adding machine
back up guitar and bass players
nod and crack jokes
behind his back
and Fidel Castro sings about love
and he sings about losing love

and he sings about finding another love
and he sings about the love he thought he'd lost
but was merely hibernating
in places he had failed to look
til this very instant
Fidel Castro spits a bit
when he sings
droplets backlit by blue stage light
reminiscent of time lapsed film
of dogwood flower
shooting pollen into the air
all the while
drummer accentuating downbeats
on cowbell muted with duct tape
and we sit at our manhole
sized table
exorbitantly priced drinks
soaking semi circles into white linen
and we listen
to this
Fidel Castro
this Fidel Castro
who in 1945
while a law student at the university
of Havana
followed
the black spike-heeled blonde
wearing that blue sequined dress
into the Tropicana Club
where he listened to Dizzy Gillespie
completely forgetting about his date
with the redhead
at the communist party meeting
this Fidel Castro
for whom music
is the revolution.

Endgame

We sit listening to a
tree frog the size of a human heart
mew like a lost cat
affixed to the dark mahogany porch post
outside your wooden slatted window
where
insects the size of candy bars
orbit around a flickering yellow light bulb
casting wayang puppet shadows
on the curtains
And you tell me the first time you were in Bali
you ran into Bobby Fischer
and I ask, Bobby Fischer the chess player?
and you say yeah
You saw him in a jazz club in Ubud
dancing to Be Bop from a keyboard, sax and drum trio
of Balinese hep cats
Skin the burnt umber color of wet clay
hair slicked back, sunglasses
a condensation of sweat beading their foreheads
smiling with teeth as even as the horizon
And Bobby Fischer is gyrating
seemingly more out of time than could be attributed to chance
And that's the beauty of it – you say
You say he wasn't dancing to the beat of a different drummer
he was dancing to the beat of *this* drummer
only in the future
Because that's what chess masters do
thinking at least three moves ahead
Bobby Fischer danced on another plane
with gusto
Hurling his arms as if he were trying to dislodge his hands
high stepping in an oscillating imaginary circle
as if marching in mud

oblivious
to anyone else on the floor
smiling as if he were about to pass out
Bobby Fischer
a man ahead of our time
not caring if we ever catch up

Balinese Dog Double Tanka

They say, in Bali,
If in this incarnation
One is not so good:
Canine the next time around
Hence, the many well fed strays

In the small grave yard
A couple dogs eye you up
But keep their distance
Like stalkers pushing limits
On a restraining order

Beondaegi

The boiled silkworm larva's flavor is not as bad as its aroma.
It offends the palette in a completely different almost subtle way,
earthen, agrarian, like dirt.
It tastes as garden soil smells at season's end,
thick tined pitchfork turning spent stalks,
wilted leaves, and fallen fruit beneath the exhausted rows
with hope of nourishing the plot for next season's seeds.

The city of Seoul's taxi drivers
refuse tips,
become offended,
even if keeping the change amounts to less than 88 cents.
The city of Seoul's taxi drivers
display their licenses permanently affixed to the right side of the
dashboard,
directly in front of the passenger seat.
Their photographs
stoically staring at their fare
are never updated.
Fresh and full of promise as a high school year book photo,
hair as black as a mockingbird's back -
skin as clear and smooth as an Asian pear,
while the man clutching the wheel
through his thin white gossamer gloves
wears a road-map of liver spots across his nearly bald head.
And I wonder,
what he and his photographed self
talk about
when driving alone.

Ducks

White cloth strips
dangle waving at the tip of bamboo rods
fifteen joint knuckled feet long
One grasped in each sinewy hand
of the Vietnamese duck man
as he steers his flock
from one rice paddy to the next
quacking foul and boisterous as
a Hanoi traffic roundabout
eating the insects that would wish
to snack on
fresh green shoots

The face of a clock
reading quarter to three
his arms soaring forward
as outstretched wings
The birds nested in the center
of the walking flock are of little concern
to the leather weathered skinned duck man
It is the outliers that he eyes
from beneath his straw non la
Those few who snap at the muslin scraps
ignoring their task at hand
spying pastures not within the constrictions
of this day's curriculum

And every good tender of livestock knows
one never plays favorites
although
how can he help but admire
the ones who push at the edges
the ones who make him work
the hardest?

Ho Chi Minh

Ho Chi Minh nee Saigon
thirty years to the day
when olive green and gray colored bats
flew from embassy belfry
flop flap flop flapping punctuation
of escape from DIY hell

At city art museum
blue silk Ao Daied attendant suggests
we begin at the top
where the past is stored
climb three flights
French provincial steps
staircase gap toothed missing ceramic tiles
yellow paint flake peeling from walls
broken stain glass repaired with plastic
Metal cage encased fan blades
spin slowly clockwise
shuffling sticky heat forward
through doorways
of vaguely lit vaulted galleries

Top floor

Greeted by Buddha bust
henna red rock chiseled
pock marked by time
sans glass case or velvet rope
braving the elements
since before Christ was born
Bronze elephant headed Hindu god
patina hand raised in peace
Decapitated wooden temple guards
torsos only swords raised

heads piked and displayed elsewhere
a fleeing conqueror's library
or antique shop
in Ho Chi Minh City, district one

Middle floor

War
Painting after painting
sculpture after sculpture
cubist realist abstract and impressionist
images
from entire generation whose children
were raised in tunnels
They the lucky ones hidden from the sun
while Dow chemical and friends
painted the jungle above into oblivion
with Napalm and Agent Orange
This artistry exhibited
as deformed fetus in glass jar
in cross town museum of the American war

Ground floor

Contemporary pen and ink
watercolor and oils of rice paddy labor
fish and stork wood block prints
Asian beauties beneath parasol
each for sale
Rendered by those who never knew
or have chosen to forget
the horrors up one flight of steps
We purchase pastel
of mischievous cats
because we find it whimsical
affordable
hoping it will match our walls
on our side of the globe

Zagreb

The streets of Zagreb's
Intestinal schematic
Swallow our rental car
As if a five Kuna coin
Picked up by curious child

Guessing at our route
We climb hills, twist through keyholes
Pray out loud for signs
But as any mother learns
Eventually, we'll pass.

Prague

účet prosim
the only Czech I mastered
"check please"
and the waiter would arrive
with the bill

shocks of stubborn grass
sea anemone anchored
in the cracks
where cobblestones
weather worn glossed
by the glow of lamplight
meets building wall
existing in plant tempo
passersby blurred
as if time lapsed photo
or Kafka's ghost
indistinguishable
from featureless
yet animate
mound of clay

účet prosim

Anchorage

The sun scarcely rises in November
shielding itself behind
mountain spiked horizon
from unremitting bitter wind
Pedestrians
wrapped as Michelin men
spend as little time necessary
outdoors
They know better than me
who
four time zones removed from home
is standing all alone
in early morning suburban driveway
breathing in
freeze dried air
and cigarette smoke
As car glides into drive
man inside
tosses plastic bagged newspaper
atop lawn concealing crusted snow
and I inquire of him
whether I am
standing too near the moose
foraging nearby
"I wouldn't get any closer"
is his reply

Coach Class

15 thousand feet nose up climbing
Houston refined to geometry
matchbox buildings
impossibly straight roadways
traffic devolving to
a pick-up truck
driven by someone
that I will never recognize
kicking dust in the middle of no where
my face
pressed against the double paned Plexiglas
scratches prism glistening
of seat 15A
flight 1232 to Chicago
and the scenery banks in response
like water in a tilted glass
as the plane turns
over the Gulf of Mexico
waves texturize the water's surface
the skin of an orange
apparently motionless from this perspective
a pattern perfect and endless
sliced by a swath of reflected sunshine
miles wide
luminescent
permanent as a fossil
from this altitude
everything
makes
sense
from this altitude
relativity sinks in

if man was meant to fly
he woulda been born with wings

Use Only as Directed...

Discontinue use of product if one or more of the following
symptoms occur
Shortness of breath and or irregular heartbeats
Sweaty palms, dryness of mouth
Delusions of grandeur
Hissy fits, conniptions, hysteria, alarm or
Blood in the stool accompanied with visions from God
Common side effects include
Imagined slights, dizziness, and abdominal cramps
Fear of the dark, ingrown hairs and constipation
In rare cases rapture has been reported
High dosages in laboratory animals has produced
Bouts of self-doubt and an inclination towards
Jumping to conclusions
In case of overdose by ingestion
Pop a paper bag behind victims back
Make three wishes administer syrup of ipecac
Bust out nearby windows and nail a bat to a north-facing wall
Respiratory protection is recommended in enclosed areas
High concentrations of vapors may produce inflammation
An uneasy feeling of malaise and acute desire
To vote Republican
Move victim to fresh air and consult physician
Skin and eye contact may result in moderate irritation
Disappointment and miniscule boils
Flush eyes for 90 minutes with goat's milk
Rinse skin with vinegar
Dress victim in their Sunday best and
March them home
This product has not been shown to cause cancer
In inanimate objects
Avoid contact with bleach, sulfuric acid and
Individuals of French decent
The information is this document

Is based on data believed to be correct
No warranty of any kind
However
Is made as to the information
In this document

911

hate is extremely flammable
its vapors may cause flash fire
hate is harmful if inhaled
keep hate away from heat, sparks and flame
do not breath the vapors of hate
wash thoroughly after using hate
if you accidentally swallow hate
get medical attention

prejudice is an eye and skin irritant
its vapors too are harmful
do not get prejudice in eyes
or on clothing
prejudice is not recommended for use
by persons with heart conditions
if prejudice is swallowed induce vomiting
if prejudice comes in contact with skin
remove clothing and wash skin
if breathing is affected, get fresh air immediately

violence is harmful if absorbed through the skin
keep violence out of the reach of children
do not remain in enclosed areas
where violence is present
remove pets and birds from the vicinity of violence
cover aquariums to protect from violence
drift and run off from sites of violence
may be hazardous
this product is highly toxic
exposure to violence may cause
injury or death.

Cookout

Arrange your ideals in a pyramid in the center of the grill.

Open your mind by pressing thumb firmly on the red dot.

Squeeze 1.6 fluid ounces of your principles per pound of belief.

Set beliefs on fire immediately.

In approximately 15 to 20 minutes or when beliefs are ashed over spread ideas evenly.

Wait 5 minutes and begin writing.

Diet

I have recently begun eating my words
Boiled they slide from the page like a pat of butter
across the bottom of a heated sauté pan
but their texture and flavor is bland
like overcooked polenta
rib spackling filling but overall
lacking
So I try again
Chopping and dicing
spicing them up with chilies and cardamom
stir frying then serving over saffron rice
They become lost in the seasoning
artifice masking for meaning
Baking I decide
three hundred and seventy five degrees
for forty five minutes only left my words dry
sticking to the bottom of the tin
So I threaded my utterances onto a skewer
An orderly syntax shish kabob
marinated in olive oil and pepper infusion
roasted over glowing charcoal briquettes
of mesquite and cherry wood

Close

but not quite good enough
for dishing up to persnickety company
Finally I just rinse them in a colander
under the tap
pile them free of pretense
raw into the wooden bowl
sitting on the countertop
to be absentmindedly snacked upon
while reading a good book

Cleanup

Time contracts
the instant glass breaks
flash freezing
for a splinter of silence
within which
all that was
that would and could be
converges into a sliver prick
of electricity

try it
throw a bottle against the wall
circus knife cart wheeling
whistle cutting through the air
flashbulb exploding and
everyone within earshot
will hold their breath
everyone
because at that moment
all bets are off

every opaque secret is laid out
like the diamond dust
of shattered windshield
across automobile hood or
the shards from
stack of diner white china
domino falling
to tile floor
behind speckled Formica counter
stopping the heart for a beat and a half
shocking bystanders
into sharp edged awareness

the everyday static

snatched away as if magician's
red checkered table cloth
bared souls teetering
long stem crystal goblets
oscillating to an upright standstill
on naked table top
when glass breaks
we reflex look inside
sans luxury of rose tinting
or UV protection
the lies we tell ourselves
that encapsulates us
in the protective vacuum
of frosted incandescent globes
become instantaneously transparent
our regrets magnified
in the blinding flare of light
before the bulb blows
our bodies paralyzed
as we stare into the cracked
mirror reflection
of our every inadequacy
for that split second
when glass breaks
but then
someone grabs a dustpan
and conversations begin again
and we live our lives
as if nothing ever happened

Schema

We are strongest where broken then mended
a weld will resist tearing surviving even the metal
that has been repaired
a stitched sail
the patch of bicycle tire tube
new soles on favorite shoes
a fractured bone
once set will knit
more resolute than before the injury

Of course
some sort of scar
a cicatrix of new connecting tissue
a slight misalignment
a stitch or a gouge
will document the lesson

The remnants of an arrowhead
in the shoulder blade
of a 5,300 year old body
of a shepherd found frozen
in the Italian Alps
the tiny white cuticle half-moon divot
beneath the right eye
of the woman with whom you are having lunch
the sealed exit of your grandfather's appendix
a mother's broken heart

Spit

So
I went to my dentist
and I asked
for my toothache back
because I missed it.

I missed the bars of light
slashing through my eyelids
like a sickle
through weeds
the sensation
of a galvanized roofing nail
piercing into and through
my sinus cavity
with jackhammer repetition
the complete inability
to piecemeal a coherent thought
I missed my toothache
and I wanted it back.

My dentist a redheaded woman
of east European accent
is convinced that I am insane

"Vut eez deese?
You go avay, come back tree munt
for cleaning

Telephone Survey

The phone rings
I answer before I finish swallowing
so
I am choking on my lunch
as I gasp I imagine
dropping the receiver
the recorded message continuing efficiently on
my skull careening off the kitchen counter
like the first bounce of a cue ball
tossed down a flight of concrete steps
I will instinctively and ever so momentarily
regain my balance
then slowly spinning on my left heel
as a pastoral paddock gate
silently swings in an early spring breeze
I list then fall onto the white tiled floor
eyes as wide as a hoot owl
the color washing from my flushed cheeks
I begin to turn blue
my dogs sit side by side in the doorway
cocking their heads in mummed amazement
while my hands become the feet of a chicken
hanging in Chinatown butcher's window
my right leg kicks as if electrically stimulated
upsetting the cat's water dish
I convulse like an automobile running out of gas
then become exquisitely still

My former dogs simultaneously cock their heads in the other
direction
the larger of the two ventures forward
sniffing as if he is reading the smells around my body
the other
jumps onto the counter
and finishes the macaroni and cheese

Just Pretend I'm Dead

Just pretend I'm dead
Just pretend I'm dead
But allow me this one luxury, see to it
that I go romantically
In a breakneck eye blink of a
"Ta ta darlings", Isadora Duncan scarf toss
beneath a red roadster's spinning tire
Better yet, entomb me in said roadster
accordion wrapped accordingly
around a bare branched sinister black oak tree
ala Ernie Kovacs, Camus or James Dean
But make sure my blood and pants are clean
free of alcohol drugs and shit
leaving no forensic clues to the mystery
of the rubber scrawled hieroglyphics on the roadway
Now I don't want no 22 caliber d.a. levy Buddha eye
or a pocketful of Marilyn's pills
You see, suicides never rate the same sympathy
and if you screw em up you just look like a jerk
No Buddy Holly blazing Cessna power dives into oblivion either
I got over that rock star thing once
I quit drinking
nope
a simple single car accident
short sweet economy

Then give me an open casket
paint it candy apple red with blue velvet lining
and have that sucker empty
Embalm me into an easy chair placed in the rear
of the viewing room
Keep my cheap cigars lit and my ginger ale fresh
so that I may enjoy my eulogies
Don't be pulling the plug on this wake

until both my ex-wives cry
and my sons have broken something
March my third grade teacher in to explain my early genius
then carry my body to Lake Erie
set it adrift on a raft made from railroad ties
and at a safe distance
blow it sky high
with eight sticks of dynamite
and I will become
food for the walleyes

Then back to my house
ransack my hard drive
read out loud
every word of writing
and weep
over its mastery
And everyone was my friend
Everyone knew me
Everyone loved me
Everyone has a story about me

Just pretend I'm dead
and give the insurance money
to whomever I am shacked up with at the time
and send them on a very long cruise.

My Wife's Laugh

I told him that
her laugh reminded me of
paint long chipped
from cracked glass
window frame in a
classroom outside of shanghai
where
quasi-legal migrant
construction worker's
black eyed children
sit
bundled
red cheeked
runny nosed
shouting
poetry
at the top of their lungs
like birds begging
in a nest

I know exactly what you mean
he replied

The Domestique

Muscle fatigue is instigated
(according to the latest scientific hypothesis)
by tiny leaks of calcium on a cellular level
stimulating enzymes to assault muscle fibers
endeavoring to shut down whatever business is afoot
but,
you already knew this

It is your nature to ignore this chemistry

Legs pumping with the precision of locomotive pistons
transferring energy to chain, sprocket and wheels
cutting through space
incited salmon-like forward
while every fiber below your neck screams
for you to stop
calves sinews braiding into knots
thighs threatening to split as if baking bread
the peloton follows in your wake
a brightly colored migration of spandex butterflies
and you come out of your saddle
to dance on your pedals
as if Bix Beiderbecke was blowing a solo in your skull
and then it comes

Your world is squeezed through a pinhole
and there is nothing
but the sound of wheels spinning
the hum of ceramic ball bearings
your heartbeat muffled in your ears
your body separates from your mind
and for an instant you are just
a projectile
sighting the finish line

Then it all explodes
shouts from the crowd first
followed by all-encompassing pain
your will cannot maintain the pace
the universe has thrown a net over you
like Moses pointing to Canaan
you signal with your elbow the sprinter
who has been riding your wheel
for one hundred and twenty six kilometers
basking in your slipstream
like a dandelion seed behind a semi-truck
and he slingshots by
to stand on the podium
to be kissed on both cheeks twice
by a duet of lovely French girls
while you look forward to Epson Salts and a whirlpool.

Beat Attitude

Blessed are those who have trouble sleeping
    For they will know the secrets of the dark
Blessed are those who have accidentally betrayed the trust of a friend
    For they will appreciate consequence.
Blessed are those whose memory is not what it used to be
    For they will not hold a grudge
Blessed are the feeders of domesticated animals
    For they will always be missed
Blessed are those who stand on the subway
    For they shall master inertia
Blessed are those who cannot read a map
    For they will never know if they are lost
Blessed are the unappreciated
    For they shall populate the earth
Blessed are the belligerently ignorant
    For they shall control all media
Blessed are those with spare change
    For they shall keep the mimes fed
Blessed are the jumpers to conclusions
    For they shall set policy
Blessed are those who cannot add numbers in their head
    For they will forever over tip

www.ingramcontent.com/pod-product-compliance
Lightning Source LLC
Chambersburg PA
CBHW051737040426

42447CB00008B/1171